The Evolution of a Saint

and Other Selected Poems

Chisaraokwu Ngozi Asomugha

WordsBuildDreams

Scripture quotations marked KJV taken from the King James
Version of the Holy Bible.

"Nne Muru Oha" first appeared in *Urban Cusp Online Magazine*

ISBN (softcover): 978-0692207314
ISBN (ebook): 978-0-9905791-0-6
Library of Congress Control Number: 2014907504

Published by WordsBuildDreams, LLC
Website: http://www.wordsbuilddreams.org
Email: info@wordsbuilddreams.org

10 9 8 7 6 5 4 3 2 1

Book Design by Jill Ronsley, suneditwrite.com

Printed and bound in the United States of America

For Daddy

Nna n'ututu k'iganu olum
K'ona arigo n'elu

This book is inspired by all those who have
been a part of the evolution—
the catalysts, the change-makers,
and (of course) the lovers. Spread love.

Contents

I   *In the beginning ...*

II   *It is not death I fear ...*

III   *So I fight …*

Preface

Sometimes evolution happens so quickly that we miss it. Other times, it is so gradual that out of shear boredom we miss the moment when change becomes irreversible and there is no turning back. Those are the moments when miracles happen—where some of our greatest lessons are learned. The title of this book comes from one of those gradual evolutionary experiences that I almost missed—not out of boredom, but out of fear. Whatever it is we face in this life, how we address it speaks to where we are in our own evolution. May the words within these pages inspire you to be present in your evolution and always learning in your life-journey. Peace and blessings to you.

—Chisaraokwu

I

"In the beginning was the Word ..."
John 1:1, KJV

Instructions for a Poetic Score in C minor

for piano solo

Piano Lover,
Try your hands upon
The ivory keys
And let them dance
A clairvoyant symphony:
Delicate, nimble
Invitingly simple,
The story of my life
In the key of C.

Master of 88 Keys,
Won't you play the mystery of me—
But when you play it,
Do so in the key of C?

Begin with a seventh
—the number of my completeness—
Then choose a ninth
to show my imperfection.
Finesse it with a dissonant minor,
though the major chord of my life
may object.
I want the sound of the unfinished
looming in the atmosphere,
anticipating what's next …

Adanne

Being the first has its privileges,
But it comes with a price.
"Make sure your siblings
Are doing alright....
They look up to you, you know."

Sometimes caught in the middle
Of being a child
and being chief-boss;
Sometimes respected,
Other times not.
The first of many:

Trailblazer!
Praised!
Adored—
"You set a good example, *Nne.*"

Who wouldn't want to wear the crown
That adorns the first daughter,
Unless, of course,
You're the first-born son ...

But that's another poem for another time.

Thick-Skinned

All black people
Are born into this world
With pale, mottled skin
But give us a day or two
Or three
And the color will come

And that's when
The skin-thickening process
Begins …

'Cause you have to be thick-skinned
To live in a society
Where your own brothers
Figure it's their right
To call you too light
Too dark
High-yella
A waste of color
Mocha
Caramel
Butterscotch
Or red-boned
And think it's a compliment
And mean it as an insult
Instead of just calling you
"Beautiful."

Body Parts

Aren't you sick and tired
Of being reduced to disenfranchised,
Disengaged,
Disadvantaged body parts
To satisfy
unenlightened philosophies
About what selfish men need
And what their hormones cannot control?

Are we not more than apple-bottom jean
Double-D wearing caricatures
Of impossible to replicate
24/7 digitalized fantasies
In stereo, surround sound and HDTV?

They reject the body of our work—
As life-givers!
As nation-rulers!
As consciousness-raisers!
And subject the wholeness of our being
To the shredder machinations
Of song lyrics and political speeches
That render the woman's body
Less than the sum of her parts.

It is an affront against our intellect,
An undeniable declaration of war!
And you want me to be okay with that?

Pleasantries

Tonight they'll ask me
about who designed my gown
who manicured my nails
who sponsored my makeup
and who the beau on my arm is.
The flashing lights of the cameras
(like Morse Code on steroids)
never savvy enough
to reveal my plans to disengage.
My smile will give them the photo they seek
To fasten their taglines to—
about how well I performed
that song that I sang
the volunteer service with the women
at the homeless shelter
The speech at that conference:
"You were so a r t i c u l a t e !"

Admirable!
Inspiring!
Tomorrow,

they'll write the headline,
"First Black Woman …"
because there are still so many things
the black woman is still first at in this country
though she was already first at it in the world,
since the beginning of time, really;
but, forgetfulness is a convenience that only they can afford.

They will converse about my upbringing
the good name I bring
pat each other on the back
shake hands in corner suites
make deals about my future.
They'll mingle with my acquaintances
that call themselves friends,
searching for that carat of information
that will render our relationship priceless.
(Those who know me will not talk;
Those who wish they did will.)

Still, in the morrow,
they'll come searching for me.
Eyeing my work
for the next big thing
to bind my name to
all before I can get a
"Good Morning, how are you?"
Because no one really wants to know
how I'm doing today.

Forgive them.
They're distracted by the possibilities
that they see in me.
Possibilities to grow their own existence
at the expense of mine.
But before the morrow,
I will have disappeared and with it their dreams.
They won't be able to find me.
Nor am I asking to be found.
And what a good morning that will be!

Diet-Crazed

I looked in the mirror today,
And my reflection asked,
"Girl, what happened to you?"
Like she didn't already know
That I'd been eating myself into a
Frenzy,
Loading up on every diet:
South Beach,
North Shore,
East Coast,
West Coast,
Compost using, eco-friendly
Vegan vegetarian
And had failed.
Yet again.

So I told her,
"... It's not like I'm trying to be an athlete!"
She smirked.
I winced.
And just like that, my motivation was gone.
My sneaky hand was sneaking snacks
Of "reduced-fat," "sugar-free" crackers
(the gluten-free kind)
While I contemplated the risks and benefits
Of walking zero point one three miles
To my local gym.

I didn't make it.
Found a soft spot on the couch

And watched "Desperate Housewives,"
'Cause I'm neither desperate nor a housewife …

I've really got to stop looking in the mirror.

Someone Knows My Name

Before the ashes of my remains
Were blown across the desert of time
I was an idea
A thought
A conceivable imagining
Worthy of contemplation
Deserving of manifestation
Innocence fashioned by Divinity's hand
Until adversity concealed my beauty
Stifled my voice
And cut off the wellspring of my soul

Echoes from the void within
Pounded against my ears
Reverberating against Nihility's walls
Making my invisibility as bright as day

Dying a thousand deaths
The thousandth and one rendered me extinct
I was no longer worth the investment
The memory of me forgotten
I became a by-word
A by-product of cultural shame

But in some I lived on
Because I was given a name:
Hope.
And though this life has rejected me,
Someone out there still knows my name.

Hi, Daddy

The western sky dressed in crimson violet
Proclaims your pending arrival
We're playing jacks on the porch
The concrete digging into the skin of our knees
The evening air crisp and light

You stroll up the driveway
In your favorite business suit
Briefcase swinging in hand
I see you

A smile appears
Jubilation
You're bigger than life—my constant
I'm lifted into your arms

Giggles escape
The smell of cologne tickles my nose
You plant a big kiss on my cheek

Daddy's home!

Siblings

The ironic manifestation
That coming from the same womb
Doesn't make you remotely similar
Even if you wish it would

The inside jokes
And outward laughter
At what parents do
To keep you in line

And ...

When broken
The only shared experience
A Name

When whole
The shared experience
Is Life

Comparative Suffering

Every time I share with you a piece of me
You let me know how you've suffered worse.
The last time I told you he beat me,
You said, "Get over it. My father beat my mom, too."

Or, like last night when I told you that the doctors
told me I have cancer. Your very first words were,
"What kind?" and I told you. You said,
"Well, it's not leukemia, so you'll be fine."

When did bitterness rob you of sympathy?
When did life's trials and triumphs become a
competition ? Maybe the issue is you …

Or, maybe the issue lies in me.
Because I keep telling you these things—
Hoping for something different.
'Cause the next day I told you
That I was going to write a book,
And you countered, "I have three editors
waiting in line to publish mine."

I love you,
but a "Congratulations"
would have been
nice.

Create Space

I'm taking a long break
From all your smothering
'Cause that claustrophobic energy
That you call love
Is messin' with my gifts
'Cause my gifts create the space
For me to grow
Gives permission for others
To walk boldly in their own
But as long as your every move
Is about how you can bend my gifts
To your will
I will have to take my gifts elsewhere
Because that manipulative *ish* ain't love, baby!
After all, the earth is big enough for the both of us.

About Isolation

We sit in too-large-for-life homes,
On cul-de-sacs of fear[1]
Removed from streets of gathering;
Manicured lawns reflecting what we covet:
Stability, security.
We posture as the learned when really
All learning happens on the outside,
In these streets of gathering,
Where rhetoric crumbles if it cannot
Stand on the foundation of application;
Where prejudice
Is ostracized because it fails
To realize the integrity
Found in the connectedness
Experienced in these streets.
Isolated from others,
Isolated from self,
This is the price we pay for our wealth.
Isolated from feeling,
Running from conversations that dispel untruths,
We no longer discern.
We are alone
In feign pristine glory.
Convinced out of our ability to commune,
Relying on years of interaction with
A reality TV real-world substitution,
Pride prohibiting us from seeking bonds,
We sit alone in our thoughts
Waiting to escape our self-imposed isolation.

---

1 Credit John DeStefano, Jr. who first used this phrase in 1993.

The Everybody Committee

Everybody's always on my case about something:
What I did or didn't do,
What I said or didn't say,
How bad I am,
Or righteous I'm not.

Just the other day,
Everybody laughed at me
'Cause I said that
One day there will be a Latino president
Whose name is José Ling!
My name is José Ling.

Everybody's out to get me;
Trying to stop my progress.
Mom says I should stop listening
To everybody. She says, "Do you, baby!"

But even when I start that,
Everybody starts talking about me again.
I wish they'd just leave me alone!

And where does Dad come off asking me,
"Just who is everybody, Son?"
WTH?!
Like I'm supposed to know everybody's name!
"I don't know," I say, putting on
My headphones to drown out the sound
Of my own discontent.

So what, if I couldn't think of their names—
They are out there!
I hear them all the time.
They're always talking.
Everybody's always talking.

Slave Masters

Behind pulpits stand preachers who
Capture the minds of men
Breed the slave-man mentality
Make dollars out of their poverty
Desiring to revive a former dynasty
In a heartless game of spirituality.

Never considering for a moment
        that
The garbage that they perpetrate
The rubbish that they vindicate
The truth that they adulterate
And preach to the masses
Is stacked like dung
Camouflaged like molasses.

Told to go teach all nations
They first reach all nations
To imprison all nations
Then rape all nations
In a name made up and sanctioned
By a dictatorship of unbelievers
Desecrators and anti-Semitics
Baptizing Judaism in Anglo waters
Mischievous counselors
Called to console
They drain the heart of humanity
And for thirty pieces of silver
They'd sell their soul.

They jockey to fill their pews
With the easy messages of convenience
But when asked the hard questions
They devise answers of cunning genius ...
With tricks up their sleeves
In the guise of suits, skirts and collars
They address only to people-please
Speaking as those learned of scholars.

Is this the Black Man's answer to over
Four hundred years of slavery—
Another millennia of
         oppression,
         degradation, and
         religious tomfoolery?

In the name of what
Do we trade one lie for another?
Black killing black oppressing black
Like black's just a color!
And still the masters get their due
Through the religion that they feed you.

While pure and true religion recognizes
The widow and the destitute,
The slave masters have turned their congregations
Into spiritual prostitutes.

II

It is not death I fear,
But the dying alone ...

II

Thoughts

"I don't believe that people lose their battle with
cancer. You know, when people say, 'oh, he lost his battle
with cancer.' Like cancer always wins and we are
losers. There are no losers. There are only fighters
and those who fight with them. And, as long as that
person's spirit remains cancer will never win. It can't
win. Because that spirit—that spirit of a brother, sister,
mother, father, cousin, or friend, that spirit that we
remember every day, every anniversary, every moment
we wish they could've shared with us—as long as
that spirit remains, then we have hope. And as long as
there's hope, we come out of this fight as winners."
#LiveStrong5

The Greatest of These

If I think for just a second too long
My head begins to spin
And my heart,
Pounding through my chest,
Forces the air out of my lungs
Before I get the chance to inhale.

Hospital rooms are always too cold.
I'm shivering and

I'm tired
But can't be more tired than you.
Laying there—
Morphine cocktails
Coursing through your veins.
The outline of your bones
Create jagged silhouettes in your skin.
You're too exhausted to talk tonight;
Too depleted to fight.

"But, who says we can't beat this thing,"
I ask, as if I'm fighting along side you.
Am I selfish to believe that we're in this together?
But we are, aren't we?
You glance at the stethoscope
Around my neck and let out a heavy sigh.

This is bullshit.
You are not losing this battle
And neither am I—
Wake up!

You shudder.
I pull the blanket to your chin
And cover your toes ...

That uncomfortable
Baby blue sofa chair next to your bed?
I collapse into it.
It's been 18 hours, 4 min and 16 seconds
Since my shift started
And I wish things were different.

You don't look at me today,
But it's okay. I remember that
We didn't place our bets
On who'd win the Sunday night football game.
The Patriots, maybe?
"The Steelers will win," I say out loud to no one.
You don't hear me.

Remember our last conversation?
You asked me why I care so much.
"Because I do," I said,
"... and, it's my job to."
You turned away, annoyed.
"Some job," you muttered.

>-+-•-◦-+-<

I've fallen asleep.
You stir.
"Hey, Doc."
The monitor beeps.
I sit up, rubbing my eyes
To bring its screen into focus.

Your breathing isn't better.

"It's time to go."

Your voice fills that space
Between life and death.

I'm not ready.
But you are.
You were always braver than I.

A Widow's Prayer

After my daddy died,
I found out my mom could pray.
Not the prayers of the Pentecostals
In tongues at high volume
Or the repetitive incantations of
Saints at Mass.
No—
These were the get down on your knees
And cry out from your soul type prayers.
The "one arrow you have pointed at me will be the
10,000 pointed at you" kind of prayers.
Straight to the point, no sugar-coating,
Prayers like
David prayed—
And he had His ear …
Those prayers that solidified her place
In the Hall of spiritual prayer warriors
Who all know the meaning of
"Touch not my anointed;
and, do my prophets no harm."

T. S. (1971-1996)

I wish you would've lived
If only that I might have seen the man
You would have become
The man you should've become
The man you were destined to be
Now
I reckon it's just a selfish unmet desire
Because when you were here
I bemoaned your brashness
Complained of your cockiness
Decried your discrimination of women like me
Suffered your sexism
And your incessant need to enter my space
And unashamedly tell your story
With and without my permission.
Perhaps
Some of my anger towards you was
Misplaced
You were what I wanted to be
Yet everything I disliked
Because you bought into their game
And played it like it was "keeping it real"
Your words betrayed you
I'd love you for a song
And hate you for a verse
Only to finally recognize—
In the lapse between bullet shot and bullet felt
Bullet taking life by force—
That I had loved you for a time
And half a time
(Romanticized as it may be)
Because your words would often speak
The thoughts that I was too afraid to own.

Until

Sterile environments never did it for me.
White walls,
White jackets,
White sheets,
A black stethoscope conspicuously draped
Around
The white neck
Of the doctor
Whose words are black
Like the cancer growing inside of me.

You can't see cancer
The way cancer sees you.
It finds all the together places in your body
And breaks them apart;
A whole you
Now broken into pieces.

⊱─━━━━━━⊰

It's just a word.
Two syllables.
But they don't roll off my tongue like they do
For the man
In the white jacket,
Leaning against a white wall,
Watching me sit on pristine white sheets
With white lights beaming from above.
He's got the wall to hold him up—
I have two syllables weighing me down.

And I'm stuck
Holding a package
That I neither wanted nor asked for
That I can't get rid of
Because the package is me,
A part of my history,
My present. My future?
I swear I was okay
Until I stepped into the darkness
In the clinic that day.

(Interlude)

I wish I could take it back,
Rewind the looks and stares,
The pity, and envy,
The helplessness:
I can't help you know how to love
Me through this—I can't help you
Know how to be present with me.
Shouldn't you already know how?
Who is strong enough to die alone?
In the Book of Life,
Make sure they include a chapter
On the loneliness of cancer.

Verse II (Thank you, K. Carr)

"I am broken" is the line in a song
That plays every moment of everyday:

Until I can erase my diagnosis,
I am broken.
Until I can stop crying long enough
To take the stupid drugs,
I am broken.

Until the belly fat is gone
And it can no longer
Predispose me to the heart attack
That could wipe me about before
Another round of cancer does,
Until I'm 5'9" and toned,
Eating organic smoothies,
And following a cancer-killing,
Anti-oxidant
Super vegan diet perfectly,
Every day,
Always, I am broken.

Until I can get a date
On a Friday night,
A Saturday night,
Or even a Monday morning
Long after remission
And the saran-wrapped existence
Of my radiation-filled days is gone
I am broken.

Cancer was the mistake that my body let happen.
Until I forgive my body—
Cancer was the mistake that my body let happen.

Until the quest for perfection
To overcome my inadequacy
In preventing the cancer
That invaded my body
Is ended, I will always be broken.
Until until happens …
But, I don't want to break anymore.

Slaughterhouse Blues

With a mic in her hand, the pastor began to address
the crowd of women seated before her. They had come
to hear her speak about trauma and domestic violence,
how to overcome exploitation.

I stood in the back of the room, listening to the call
and response echoing through the chamber: Mm-hmm's
issuing from lips, heads nodding, rallying her on. I
wondered if they were really listening to her, or were
they simply entranced by the rhythm of her voice?

The gentle waves of affirmation erupted into a chorus
of amens and thunderous applause as she said, "You
need Jesus to help you with your problems … not a
shrink!" She pleaded with them to "go to church."

I wept.

Because Christians never needed a shrink and holiness
is the only way to fight depression, anxiety and PTSD?

Sigh.

I long for the day when shepherds no longer lead their
sheep to the slaughter …

Foggy Bottom

Like an anvil
Pressed with the full weight of gravity
Upon your head
Like an intense throbbing
That pulsates with every
Anxiety-ridden second of existence
Such is the foggy mind.

Like that tension
Created in the tug of war
Between your soul and your mind
As if from the hairs on your head
To the toes of your feet
You are being stretched to your breaking point
Until your body is as thin and invisible
As the horizon
Such is the yearning of a foggy mind.

Devoid of all things vivid
With diminishing capacity to dialogue in color
It becomes isolated
Misunderstood by others.
It seeks but never finds the sun above the clouds.
It misses its own smile.

Its instinct is to depart from
Holier-than-thou prayers of saints
That end with "Get over it."
So it sleeps in the wake of

Loud expectations
Harsh criticisms
Bully pulpits
And the beguiling deceipt
Of those who call themselves friends.
Because there is no "Amen" for the brokenhearted.

O, that its desire to commune could be heard,
Would you draw it out of hibernation?
Would you note that flicker of yellow
in a sea of gray—an invitation?

O, that you would know her heart
Her love
Her thirst for light.
Would you speak with her
And watch the sun rise?

Over-Medicated

Crack never hurt nobody
That was already dead
Even if their spirits
were alive enough
To know that
They would rather die
Then live invisible
In the shadows
Of the policy wonks
Who dictate their future—
Our future

Listen!
The boys on my block
Smoke weed
'Cause the world
Can't hear them sobbing at night
When the belt hits their backs
And the pain of teachers
Telling them their too lazy
Rings in their ears

My belly swells with fear for them!
Who's going to love them out of
Their haze-induced melancholy?

Listen!
The bottle became my friend
When foe was a partner
That came in the guise of love
But pushed a black and blue hurt

On my body temple instead—
And a morning hangover
Means I survived the night

Listen!
My sisters play tricks
At the local park
In the light of day
The sounds of their illicit activities
Rise above the squeals of children at play
'Cause this is the way to survive
The lonely path ahead
For a black girl like me

You tell us what you think we need to succeed,
But you won't listen!
You don't understand:
We aren't looking for a pill to fix us;
We're looking for a place to disappear into.

Therapy Sessions

Against walls painted olive green
Hang the faces of children I will never know.
Were they yours or mine?
Did we have them together, or
Were they from a previous life ...?

Today, I'm curious ...

My fingers,
Loose fingers
Fidget. Uneasiness inspires them to pick loose
The piece of string on the orange terry-clothed
Chair   that I am sitting in ...

*"How about you tell me what you're thinking about
right now?"*

The rain falls hard today.
The silver lining in the sky
A long procession of ominous clouds
Marching towards me,
Daring me to stare them down
Through my windowpane.
I hide, instead, in the aegis of a dark corner
Behind neatly discarded memories
Waiting for the storm to pass.

Her question searches me out.
I had hoped to tell her the truth,
The truth that slips out unfiltered
Even if it doesn't make a sound.

A truth so fiery red that it burns
Its story onto my heart every time
My brain wishes to forget.

They were my children after all … not hers.
What business does she have searching my thoughts?

I wonder if she knows what I'm thinking
But doesn't have the heart to tell me.
Maybe she's like me:
The truth is much harder to hear,
So we ask the questions
That we already know the answers to.

Wake-Keeping

A child's silent cries.
A whisper in the dark.
Unable to articulate or fight,
He curls himself into a ball,
Protecting his heart
From the beatings that press against him.
He has learned that he can handle the pain
Better than most.
So he unwillingly, unknowingly invites your issue
To be his issue
Until he no longer can feel his presence—
Forgotten, abandoned
Questioning his very identity and existence.

What Mourning Is

To be clear:
Mourning is not insanity.
It's for those who love and love fiercely,
For those who believe in relationships and relating,
For those who know the depths
and heights of passion,
Who know the anguish and fear of loss.

Mourning is for those who know happiness
and the exhilaration of peace,
Who live in the moment and
celebrate what is and is to come.

It is not a sign of weakness,
A giving up of dreams,
Nor is it a sign of peril or defeat.
It's an acknowledgement,
An acceptance and affirmation of what was—
No matter how beautiful or ugly it may have seemed—
that what we had was good
for the time we had it.

So when you mourn the loss of a dream
A love or lover, a season or other,
Don't let them hold back your tears,
or stifle your cries,
Like you are beyond your own humanity!
As if they lack the understanding
That life will no longer be the same!

Those who have not known
What it means to love and lose greatly,
To walk down the aisle, no father in tow,
To lose children not yet ready to die,
To yearn for the destiny
That had anchored your soul and watch it slip way—
can they instruct us on how to wear our mourning?

Rather than pretend that we cannot feel,
Let us mourn the loss
And celebrate the time.
Let us cry until our eyes are spent,
Our voices hoarse,
Our anger has reached a fever pitch and subsides,
Our questions are wrestled with,
And our praise has reached the farthest corners of the
heavens!
Let us wail with all that we have
For there is strength in our tears.

And when we are through with our mourning,
Let us rise in the morning—
In all of its splendor—
Dust ourselves off,
Put on our regalia of hope,
And celebrate what is and is to come.

Pedestals

Atop the mountain of emptiness
We idolize our deepest fears
The disquiet of our souls
Driving us to hide behind
Beguiling specters of what we should be
Fallacious rhetoric about how we could be—
(Ever) presenting perfection
Denying our blessed humanity

We live upon the pedestals
Of our trepidation
Rising higher to escape our truth

The fall is great
From the heights of our insecurity.

Connecting

Connection is what happens when
Discipline is no longer a substitute for strength
Rigidness no longer trumps love
Righteous works do not equate acceptance
Self-made boundaries and scheduled talks
No longer prohibit us from engaging in real talk
You and I talk—
Without the constructs
Moving freely into My dwelling place
No longer misguided by who you think I am
And how we relate.
True connection is you seeing Me as I AM,
Just as I have always seen you as you are—
Fearfully and wonderfully made.

Walk on Water

It's the New Year's Eve.
Torrential downpour
Is expected.
The threat
Of home being washed away
Makes me queasy.

But it's the night before the New Year!
Come celebrate with us!

Of course, I must show up
To the party and engage in frivolities.
(It is in my honor, you know.
After all, don't we all ignore
the weatherman's predictions?)
All while my home teeters on the water's edge.

"River will crest above flood stage tonight"
the morning paper read ...
Run is what I want to do.
Run and hide, in the attic.
The water won't find me there.
I don't swim.

Wine glasses cling
The music stops

Speech! Speech! Speech!
Rehearsed speak: *It's the end of the year!*

What people want to hear
Is the overcoming and passing through.
To float upon resolute choruses
That usher in newness in
Old and tattered rags.
Always about how it'll be different
This time, except that it's not.

Above the din of late night chatter
The steady drumbeat of rain morphs
To a persistent knocking upon my soul.
(Time blurs our perfunctory gab and
impersonal air kisses into a weightless,
unmeasured symphony that tonight
I am too burdened to conduct.)
The imponderable urge
To divulge without script,
The inner workings of a jaded heart
And cluttered spirit-mind billow,
Breaking through. I give in.

This deluge—
An uncensored and vulgar beauty
Casting light upon every
Judgment and condemnation
Upon the call & the Caller
The beginning, middle and ending
Of a sanctimonious life
Unfiltered,
Unabashed—
Washes over me.
then us.

Silence.

I'm out in the middle of the ocean,
Standing alone.
Un-burdened I am—
A lighthouse signaling to me in the distance—
As I walk towards the shore.

Amnesty

I used to think if I cursed you out,
Things would change.
Or maybe if I could get you to see
Beyond your own nose,
Things could change.
Better yet, if I could make pigs fly,
Give you ribbons in the sky,
Or make hell freeze over,
Things would change.

After all, aren't these the things
of forgiveness?
I give and you take and the world
is okay again?
But it is not.

Forgiveness is the acknowledgment
of our fallibility:
Loving ourselves more than the injury;
Letting die what could have been;
Accepting past and present,
And burying dead weight
Because carrying it never made anyone
more alive.
It is the funeral service
for unmet expectations and lived hurts.
Liberating us from the prison cell
of guilt and shame and setting
our spirits free.

ReCreation

Tattered Torn Used Run-over ...
You take pieces
And bring together
Artwork Exquisite Gems
Singular Individual
Invaluable Strong
Unbreakable
Yours.

III

"So I fight,
not as one who beats the air ..."
1 Corinthians 9:26, KJV

The Evolution of a Saint

When the world was fashioned,
The three-legged stool that I sat on
Gave way and down a rabbit-hole
of fear I fell. I found my resting place
in your dogma.

Don't tell; don't touch; I shall not
Love you. Like a virgin in heat,
For your affection I would tarry
in black and white,
in power and in might,
in hopes your glance would find its rest
on my person. You were beautiful,
awe-filled to me. I read
your song of Songs and
mastered your words
and actions. Did I not preach
your love to the masses?

You decreed: to have and to hold—
I was your muse,
Until what you had and held
was no longer me,
and I could no longer find
myself in the fantasy, or
maybe it was I who willfully
played Creator. You, after all,
were made in my image,
once upon a time ...

I had prayed to find the right path
Back to you. Labored with cross
And crown 'til blood was spilt
on unhallowed ground. Our blood—
that tied us together,
that forgave us the sins
we committed against each other!
You carried me in the hole of your heart
with little left to feast from but
the caries that had eaten away at
the core of you. And yet hungry,
I still labored to be the whole that would fill you,
ached to be the sum of your parts—
if only to cover the shame
of my inability to entice you
to love me.

You stood with me when
The ground shook the first Time.
You called me your own: *Nkem.*
I inhaled you in that moment—
like oxygen to my organs
you refreshed me; and, I exhaled
the fear of losing you.
You and I.
Nightly prayers,
Sunday morning check-ins,
and a preacher to play mediary
between me and your son.
That time, you left behind your kisses
so that I would remember the taste of you.
I searched for you and you found me.
But when the ground shook again,
You were gone—

And, with you, our eulogy on your lips.
The gods were angry that night.
Their lurid appetites filled the night air,
eating away at any semblance of divinity
left in me. The stars illuminated like
the Anointed One's body on Calvary
at that moment when the curtains rent in two
and you were through with living
in my box. —The heavens released
their fury in a thunderous cloudburst.
Numb, disoriented, I tasted
the salt of my tears.
Where is my North Star?
Did he not see me? Has he forgotten
his first love? With what light will
I find my way back to you?

Lost between past and present,
Unsure of eternity,
I cried out no name but yours.

><

"I love you" is foreign to my lips
But to your ears they are life.
But what is life for me?
For what cause did I lay on this altar
With no ram in the bush for my sake?

O! burdensome love—How I wanted to fix you
For the fixing the world had given me!
What would they have said if I let You be?
What would they have said if I let US be?

><

Ha Ruach found me on Straight Street
Twisted from the knottiness of
Life, disconnected from
my beating heart later discovered
in a place long neglected for
simple want of redundant
rituals of purported love and praise,
rather than the ebb and flow of grace,
the back and forth of Relationship.

———

It was a Monday when we met again.
A lifetime had passed since
I had gazed upon your beauty,
since I had first heard you speak my name.
No one else had understood our relationship—
such remarkable insensibilities we exuded!
An unlikely pair, you and I; but, you spoke
love to my captivity
and made freedom my daily bread
until it massaged my voice from out under
my fear
and I could sing our song again ...
We danced a gentle waltz around its lyrics,
feeling our way around and within each
other. I, learning to trust your lead; you,
waiting for me to let go.

We are closer, you and I,
For want of each other as we are.
No longer adhering to what others
deem necessary for understanding.
I pay sweet attention
to your voice, the words

that unearthed my preconceived notions
of you, of me
and blew them away as ash.
I am whole again,

for the first time. I am found.
Love is a shapeless fluid
that wills away confinement;
abhors control. A tenderness that
chips away at feign order; it is
the pardon for living by the book
and not by the heart; the clemency
for wearing perfection instead
of authenticity. It is the beginning
and end of my evolution—
For in it, I am human. I am
saint. I am complete and at
peace. Perfect peace.

Humility

Every time you think you understand
Make sure to remind yourself that you don't.
The moment you think you know it all
Is the moment you lose your best asset:
Your ability to grow.

Poetry in Limbo

It's a *fad* to read poetry like a song
With "blackness" all around you
And afro-disiacs hailing you ...
As if to be considered a true poet
One must make hips sway
And lips sing a cacophonic blend of foolishness
Inflicted on the masses.
The sanctity of words lost
In the performances of mediocre stage wannabes
Who think that words are best expressed
From mouth and not heart, just 'cause.

Black, *brown, white* poetry before a mic
Placed on a stage by socialites
Who only search out fame and fortune
Never having lived shame or misfortune.
Hoping to be the next slam poet/rap artist ...
Yet, too scared to understand the struggles
That brought the poet
To where she knows that "it"—
This whole poetry thing—
Is not really about the performance
But about the Words
The journey that brought the Words
The emancipation that came from the Words
Flowing on paper
Over invisible microphones
On full blast to the world
In its purest form: Life.

For Ms. Sabrina's Girls (Morning Devotion)

Before I was formed,
He clearly determined
That I would possess
The strategies and paradigms
That would define
And refine my existence—
Establishing
      new ideas of
          achievement,
              ever-debunking the status quo!
I,
no longer an afterthought,
would Personify
new thought unparalleled.

Heaven-sent,
down-to-Earth,
Freely birthing ingenuity
With quiet confidence,
Using gifted hands,
And genuine heart to build
society,
nationhood …
community.

Previous formulaic calculations
Of what I should have been
Dispelled instantly
In the richness of an experience
Primed through adversity—

My eloquence and poise
Born through creativity.

I am a Masterpiece
Among all creation:
Bridging and connecting
All of humanity
In the bold and vibrant ways
That the world
And you
And I need.

This Is for You (On the First Day)

I am not an accident.
BIG BANG did not spit me out into the cosmos.
I was not created as an amoeba
And did not evolve into a human being.
My ancestors were not apes hanging from trees.
They had names like yours: William, John and Mary.

I am not an experiment gone wrong
But a thoughtful creation done right.
Because He knew that I would be a force
To be reckoned with,
He gave me a name—The Answer.

The answer to every man's questions
And ignorant philosophies that claim
My hips are not wide enough
My lips are too thick
My stance not black enough
My fight not right
My soul not strong enough.
And yet in His image He created I.

So, I live the answer—
Not for their understanding,
For in all their getting
They have lost themselves.
But for those who came before me
And for those who will come after me,
Who will question the logicians and
Scientists who will attempt
To pollute their minds with theories

Of the culture of poverty
Or the media moguls
With their aspirations of impossible beauty
And the need to be too thin to survive
And too gangsta to live another day.

—Living for me and those
who do not wish to die trying,
But want to live doing ...
Doing greatly
With purpose,
Not by accident.

On the Eighth Day

In the event that you find yourself
Caught between salvation and dogma,
Take two steps back,
Close your eyes and sing.
That's right: sing.
Sing loudly!
Because the devil don't like singing
And when you sing
        he gets angry.
Sing the song of your ancestors
Who cried for home!
Sing the song of their prayers
That split floating coffins
With human cargo
On a wide open sea
        In two
Because freedom in death
Is better than captivity in the unknown!
Sing your way out the doors
Of personified strongholds and
Righteous legalism
Into a carefree noonday!
And most important of all:
        Carry a sword.
The sword will come in handy
When you will inevitably
Have to cut off the tentacles of
Church folk desperate to choke
Out your essence
As you walk into your freedom.

Antebellum
(We need another war like we need another televised Revolution ...)

When I was 15 years old, I told him that *if I had grown up in the sixties, I might have been a Blank Panther ...* 'cause they were fierce, dressed in all black, did what the government would not do and demanded respect ... and he laughed because I was a woman who had not yet read up on the misogyny that existed within their ranks ... but still I admired what it represented to me: that the oppressed can rise up in solidarity, that they could join arms with others and demand equality ... and do it wearing afros and dashikis! You can't ignore that!

The Revolution

I'm not talking about *that* revolution—
About race, class or gender—
I'm talking about

That revolution that starts from within,
That doesn't negate the color of our skin,
But leads us deep inside our hearts
To be liberated from the prison of our sins—
The sins that made us hurt ourselves,
And love what they had instead of our selves,
That caused us to close our eyes to the
Trauma inflicted against and by us,
That stopped us from being united for good,
Expressing our love for one another
In the name of all that is righteous.

A revolution too hard for some to swallow!
It lacks the luster of the fight of the oppressed—
The Red, the Black, the Poor, the Yellow.
Not sexy enough to be televised,
Nor violent enough to be glorified.
Yet, the violence inflicted
By denying our own humanity
Continues to oppress us by the virtue of the walls
We have built with the bricks of separation
And the mortar of our fears.

How long will we keep fighting to be different
When our purpose is the same?
Don't we all dream?
Don't we all cry?
Don't we all pray?

The time is now for an uncompromising
People who will rise up
To claim their inalienable right
To inhabit the earth freely,
To live their greatest selves boldly,
With voices chanting freedom's song,
And the rhythm of united hearts beating—
Allies assembled
Indivisible
Extolling excellence
Breaking down strongholds
Establishing peace
With unity and justice for all.

Can you feel it?

WarSpeak

Gingrich says
      there's a war on religion

Something about how the President's destroying
Some forefather's vision written
On a piece of paper back when
I couldn't have
      Written this poem
      Without hiding in the dark
      In the corner of a room
      My pen, a piece of bark
            That would later be used to lash my
            back and
            Grow a different kind of tree
            To create paper from
            Whose pages would tell a different
            story

    But not about religion

Something about a war on religion
And the battlefield is my body
In the balance
A judicial decision
About when I can protect my temple-body
From what's unwanted
      Because of a misguided hand
      That lay hold of my neck
      And forced his way in
      Before I could scream
      That would later come back to haunt me

With the shame of a sin
That was not my own
(Yet, I'm the one being cross-examined
In front of the President's men)
But I couldn't tell the story

Religion is not about the story

Some thing this war on religion is
    That makes grown men blind
    To my *his*tory
    'Cause even his words insert themselves
    into my story
    Becoming the law
    Without my consent

No, there's no war on religion, Sir.
Religion has never been at war with us
Nor did it create the weapons
To destroy the spirit of humanity
That are used daily to subjugate those you call
"Other."
It was man who created the dubious piety
That would war against our ability
To exist peaceably within our differences.

The real war is the war against my freedom:
Freedom to choose
Freedom to live
Freedom to exist in peace and not in pieces!

I AM

I am woman coming of age
Having exchanged my minimum wage
For an inheritance of nobler sage
Refined sass
Flowing through me
I am masterful in artistry
Compassionate in delivery
A living proverb—
Chapter, verse and psalm.

I am hot like fire
Calm like moment before the storm
Remembered like the words
"I have a dream"
Present like the dream personified
I am here.

I am born again
Into a righteous family
Daughter of the land of the rising sun
Of a people called to walk in liberty
Shackles of colonial mischievousness
Broken that we would forever be free
I am their song.

At the corner of my past and my future,
I am reborn.
Gazing into a searing sun,
I am renewed.
Spewing forth resurrection knowledge

Life-giver   Lover of Life
I have become a new creature
I am now.

To be or not to be
Is not my question
For not to be would cease for me
The realization of my manifest destiny
This piece of my culture is
The peace of me
Master this piece spiritually
For I am His handiwork.

The embodiment of beauty and strength
Diligent in all of my business
Caught into the third and fourth heavens
Taking this my daily bread
I am deliberate in my haste
My cup runneth over
Surely His goodness is with me
And because He is, I AM.

The New Poor

The new poor are not impoverished
They did not lose their jobs
Or their savings
Or grow up in the segregated landscapes
Of our nation's poor.
Indeed they are well-off,
Educated,
And greedy.

They live in fear
Wired to want and want
But are never satisfied.
Only seeking friendship for gain,
Amassing followers like currency,
Celebrity like it's a low-risk investment,
Confusing fame for family.
Their emptiness reveals
The scarcity in their pockets.
Filling up on the materials of life,
With a hole in the bottom of their souls,
They wonder why they never have enough.
Bankrupt they are.

But the poor will always be with us.

For Papa John, Father James, Uncle Ben and Mr. Jefferson (a.k.a. Sally's Man)

We hold these truths to be self-evident
That brokered deals on Wall Street never brought
The poor man a profit on Main Street
That glorified ghetto slums
Are the dreams turned nightmares
Of romanticized plantations
And 1960s gentrification
Turned 21st-century modernization
At the expense of an entire population.

Prolific writers of caste systems
Concealed and memorialized
By tablet and pen
Having scripted another man's mortality
Without questioning
Always believing
They died wondering
Who will ever determine
How three-fifths can become a whole?

But we the change-makers
In order to form a more righteous Union
Establish a new declaration of independence
From the dependence on foreign demagogues and
Imagery about who we are and what our names
Should be, from those who play us like a fiddle in an
Anti-*christos* symphony.

'Twill be an amaranthine creed past down
From generation to spiritual generation
This era's emancipation proclamation!
No longer sustainable
To dismiss as undeniable our destiny.

For in the course of these human events
We have found our voice with *biro* and paper
Smartphone and tablet
To undo the offenders
And cast off the blasphemous
And embrace new knowledge
True knowledge
Of the spirit, by the spirit and through the spirit.

Amen!

Nne Muru Oha

Practically irreverent
Flying high above the landscape
Soaring freely
Through the aerospace of divine magic
She's limitless

Eyes that gaze with tender grace
A golden tongue that sings
Rhapsodies of love and life
Composed in psalms of spring

In peaceful chaos, quiet noise
She whispers melodies
That transform life's mundane-ness
To an awe-filled Technicolor dream

With strength to move mountains
She glides across valleys
Her feet unearth new revelations
And up above her head treasures are found

She drops the seeds of wisdom today
That will sprout life tomorrow
Their eternal imprint
Justifies her legacy

She is the first and the last
Beginning and always
The why and how
The what and is
The you
The me
The woman of life she be.

Beyond the Cross

She won't trust the Buddhists
With their statues and meditation
And he can't find the hundred
and one-half Scriptures
That tell you to meditate
So they dismiss the incantations
Of the devout as superstition.
But they will be the first
To hold up their cross
Tie it around their neck in gold
And say a prayer
To a man they have never seen
Call him by a name
That isn't even his
And claim to be more holy.

The religious all have their symbols,
Their statues and their vows.
Some trust in chariots and others in horses.
But the children of YAH—
They have *relationship*.

On Religion

Religion is a complicated thing
It will get all up in you
Make you seek perfection
While shaming you into failure
It has many followers and dictators
And holy-ghost shouters ...
But that intangible thing
That gets you up in the morning
Seeking wisdom prayer and counsel
That embraces your imperfection
Shows strong through your weakness
Removes your shame
Covers you in love
And calls you by name?
That's Relationship—
No religion has power over that.

To Be Continued ...

I read somewhere that "anybody can die for a noble cause," but the sign of maturity is "to live day by day for the cause." I have only lived a short while on this earth, but I've seen what we can do. We believe we can go to the moon and send someone to live there. We believe we can lock ourselves in a metal tube with wings and fly six miles above the earth to nearly any destination in the world. We believe we can communicate with people in remotest parts of the earth over invisible airwaves ... We've done that. We did that. We do that. But we don't have the conviction to change our communities and reduce gun violence, empower our youth even if they are too young to vote, have equity across all groups regardless of our perceived differences, or to acknowledge that mental illness is real. It's not rocket science, people. We can keep shooting for the moon; but the more we look to the moon for the answers, the less energy we'll have to travel into the depths of our souls, find the connection within us all, and carry out the revolution that this world needs.

Peace.

ACKNOWLEDGMENTS

To my Creator, YAH, who loved me into being. To my inspiring family who reminds me every day of what is truly important. To Patricia Harris-Boyce, Dr. Rhonda Maddox, Pierce Minor, Amaka Unaka and Dr. Ndidi Unaka: Thank you for answering the call! Finally, to those past and present, who have inspired these words and have shaped my evolution: love and peace. Words build dreams.

www.ingramcontent.com/pod-product-compliance
Lightning Source LLC
LaVergne TN
LVHW040053090426
835513LV00028B/594